A Warrior's Blessing and other meditations

Tony Brady

"Do not believe in anything simply because you have heard it. Do not believe in anything simply because it is spoken and rumored by many. Do not believe in anything simply because it is found written in your religious books. Do not believe in anything merely on the authority of your teachers and elders. Do not believe in traditions because they have been handed down for many generations. But after observation and analysis, when you find that anything agrees with reason and is conducive to the good and benefit of one and all, then accept it and live up to it."

- Buddha

Copyright © 2017 Tony Brady

All rights reserved.

ISBN-13: 978-1979310888
ISBN-10: 1979310882

DEDICATION

This work is dedicated to the creators, designers and contributors to the wonderful Insight Timer App who have inspired me to produce these meditations for the App which in turn prompted me to offer these reflections in book form for the benefit of those who might wish to read them. Let us all do what we can to encourage one another. But in all this remember the advice of the Buddha: Do not accept anything simply because someone else has told you so. Check the evidence, try the remedy offered and see for yourself if it accords with your own reason.

May you be well.

May you be happy.

May your life be blessed.

Tony Brady – Dublin – October 2017

ACKNOWLEDGMENTS

I acknowledge with gratitude the people whose works and quotes are briefly referred to in this book and I hope that the short extracts included here will encourage you to explore further the writings of the authors concerned.

CONTENTS

1 - THE TAPESTRY OF LIFE 1

2 - PRAISE AND BLAME 7

3 - GATEWAY TO SLEEP 9

4 - A SHORT LITANY OF THANKFULNESS 15

5 - MEMORIES OF HAPPINESS 19

6 - A BLESSING FOR YOU 23

7 - AWAKE THE DAWN 27

8 - GATEWAY TO EMPATHY 33

9 - SUPPORT IN A TIME OF BEREAVEMENT 39

10 - A KEY TO HAPPINESS 49

11 - MEDITATION TECHNIQUES 53

12 - SLOWING AND STOPPING 57

13 - WE ARE BLESSED TODAY 65

14 - FOR TODAY, JUST LET THINGS BE 71

15 - GRATITUDE FOR A NEW DAY 75

16 - GRATITUDE FOR WATER 79

17 - A GRATITUDE WALK DOWN MEMORY LANE 85

18 - WHY KNOCK YOURSELF? 91

19 - WHEN WILL WE BE AWARE? 97

20 - IN TIMES OF FEAR AND UNCERTAINTY 101

21 - YOU ARE A TODAY'S GIFT TO THE WORLD. 109

22 - YOU ARE UNIQUE 117

23 - TAKE BACK YOUR ON-LINE LIFE 123

24 - A WAVE OF BLESSING 129

ABOUT THE AUTHOR 134

A final word: 134

1 - THE TAPESTRY OF LIFE

In the course of each of our lives, many people will come and go.

Some people enter, and they stay with us for the whole of a lifetime. Other people accompany us for only for a short while.

Our lives are, in that sense, like a train journey with passengers getting on and off the train as it moves from station to station.

In this meditation, we think of how we might reflect with mindful compassion on our lost friends, the people who have been part of our lives and who, for one reason or another, have moved on.

Francis Thomson tells us:
"The fairest things have fleetest end,
Their scent survives their close:
But the rose's scent is bitterness
To him, that loved the rose."

TONY BRADY

We can at times be feeling sad because people who were once part of our lives are no longer with us. Death, of course, is something over which we have no control. Sadness at the loss of a loved one is natural, and we must expect that we will, over time, lose people through death.

But what we wish to look at here is the loss of people through the breaking up of relationships and friendships or the process of merely drifting apart as the paths of our lives diverge.

I invite you to spend one minute, just 60 seconds, thinking of some people whom you have lost, not because of death, but simply through the changing circumstances of life.

Please don't allow yourself to become fretful about the people concerned. This pause is just an invitation to call people to mind so that you might better cope with the fact that they are no longer part of your everyday life.

We could spend time vaguely regretting the fact that we seem to have drifted apart from someone. Perhaps someone crosses our mind, and we loosely wish we could renew the old acquaintance. Now if we desire that a relationship might be re-established, someone has to make the first move, so maybe you might decide today to take such an initial step in the next little while.

A WAVE OF BLESSING AND OTHER MEDITATIONS

Pause to consider if your first move is what is appropriate concerning any of your lost friends as you read this.

If you feel that someone has been allowed to drift away, and you feel the inclination to try to re-establish contact, resolve to approach the person very soon, if possible in the next week, while the thought is fresh in your mind,

In the course of a lifetime, many people will separate from us merely through busyness or even neglect. In some cases, the split arises because someone no longer gets on well with us and we no longer see eye to eye with them.

There need not have been a major disagreement. There may of course in some cases have been a deliberate parting of ways, but more usually it is just that they - or we - have taken a path in life that is different one from the other.

Although in a general sense we wish everyone well we cannot be friends with every person we meet. There is a limit to the number of people we can each fit into our lives in any significant way. Any of us will be lucky indeed if we can count on the fingers of one or two hands a set of people who genuinely love us, and we them, in any meaningful way.

So, for the people who have moved on or moved apart from us, let us we see if we might, with love, compassion and gratitude consider them to be part of the tapestry of our lives and let them go.

Let us try to quench any bitterness we might feel at their departure.

Wish them well.

Give thanks for the fact that, for a time, they were part of our lives and we were part of theirs.

A suggestion is that we would place the names of people who are on our minds in this way into a memory box. Just the names, not the details. Then, occasionally, we might take that box into our hands, open it, mindfully look through the names of former friends and quietly say:

I give thanks for the fact that each of these people was part of the tapestry of my life.

I am sorry for any suffering I may have caused any of them.

I forgive any suffering that any of them may have caused me.

I wish them well.

I wish them happiness.

I wish them peace.

I hold no grudge against them.

I hold them in the light of grateful remembrance.

In some situations, even though it may not be easy to put an end to some residual bitterness we might feel, it is crucial that we try to let go.

Forgiveness will benefit you more than the person against whom you feel a grudge.

Forgiveness is not something we do for others. Forgiveness and letting go is something we do for ourselves.

Not forgiving someone is the equivalent of staying trapped in a jail cell of bitterness, serving time for someone else's crime.

There is a popular song entitled *"If you really love her let her go."*

The Vietnamese Peace Activist Buddhist monk Thich Nhat Hahn says *"Letting go gives us freedom, and freedom is the only condition for happiness. If, in our heart, we still cling to anything - anger, anxiety, or possessions - we cannot be free."*

So, in gratitude, stand back, observe the tapestry of your unique life. Looking at those people who were, but are no longer, part of it:

Wish them well.

Wish them happiness.

Wish them peace.

Hold no grudge.

Hold each of them in the light of grateful remembrance.

Remember the reality that they have walked part of the road of life with you.

We might usefully call to mind the serenity prayer which will be a help when it comes to deciding whether we should try to renew an old acquaintance or, instead, in a spirit of thankfulness and a spirit goodwill, assign the name of that individual to our memory box.

> *"God, grant me the serenity to accept the things I cannot change,*
> *Courage to change the things I can,*
> *And wisdom to know the difference."*

2 - PRAISE AND BLAME

Lao Tzu tells us *"Be still; stillness reveals the secrets of eternity."*

So in response to this piece of wisdom let us find now a moment of stillness, a moment of quiet calm.

Just breathing in - just breathing out.

Just breathing in - just breathing out.

In this reflection, we take a look at praise and blame.

Some days people will praise you, and you will feel great.

Others will criticise you, and you will go to pieces.

But who knows the true you?

Who knows the effort you make?

Who has walked even a short distance in your shoes?

So from now on when you receive praise, take just a little credit.

It is possible that you deserve some of it.

When you hear criticism, take just a little of it on board.

Even a stopped clock is right twice a day.

But don't seek re-assurance or approval. Our need for these fleeting and feeble opinions can never be satisfied.

Bear in mind that even you do not fully understand the mystery that is the inner you.

For today just do your reasonable best.

Your best is a straightforward measure.

And having done your best, sleep well when this day is done.

The same tomorrow.

It will add up to a good life,

With you the judge.

3 - GATEWAY TO SLEEP

This reflection is designed to help you enter into a relaxed mood before you go to sleep.

Some people have difficulty getting to sleep. For others, a five-minute sit before the TV, or the reading of five pages from a book is all they need to bring about a feeling of drowsiness before slumber overtakes them.

Other people are worried about one thing or another, and for them, it might be helpful to note the words of John Steinbeck who says this:

> *"It is a common experience that a problem difficult at night is resolved in the morning after the committee of sleep has worked on it."*

Very true words. Remember that in the comfortable cocoon of sleep we often find the solution to many of our problems. The counsel "sleep on it" is a wise suggestion.

So can you bring yourself into a state of relaxation?

Become aware of your breath, your breathing in and breathing out.

As you breathe out can you think of the words *"Just let things be - just let things be."*

Do you notice any tension in your body? Bring your awareness to it and see if you can manage to let it go with the thought, *"For now just relax - for now just relax."*

It may help to release tension in your body if you can tighten up the problem part and then release and let it go.

You might like to try this by doing a body scan. In a body scan you start at your feet, and you tighten up and then relax each part in turn until you reach your face and head, where, one again, you give a big scrunch and then allow a significant letting go of the tightness.

Next I would like you to turn your attention to your mind and notice what is going on after the challenges of the day.

Just as we need to relax our bodies, so -and even more so - do we need to quieten our minds.

We have so many thoughts spinning around, regurgitating

the past, planning how we will respond to words yet to be addressed to us in the future, speculation about things that might never happen.

Mark Twain once said, *"I've had a lot of worries in my life, most of which never happened."*

Naturally, we have to take lessons from the past and work to bring about the future we desire, but that is active thinking and real action in the here and now, not wasting the present by regretting the past and not ruining our future by ignoring what we need to do in the present.

Sleep is an excellent restorative.

Shakespeare describes it as *"the innocent sleep."*

He puts it beautifully when he says that sleep knits up *"the ravelled sleeve of care",*

Let us allow sleep to knit up our ravelled sleeve of care,

He goes on to call it *"sore labour's bath",* that beautiful image of lowering our bodies into warm water at the end of a busy day.

He describes sleep as the *"balm of hurt minds."*

He tells us it is

"great nature's second course, chief nourisher in life's feast."

And realise also that rest is every bit as good as sleep.

Some people who find it difficult to get to sleep, generate anxiety with the effort and that very anxiety prevents them falling asleep.

My suggestion is that you try to fix a regular calming pre-bed-time routine and, as you go to bed, see if you can express gratitude for the many gifts of the day.

Generate feelings of goodwill towards the people in your life. Then let rest, and hopefully sleep, arise naturally as a result of your quietly resting in that happy state.

So as an exercise just now see if you can recall with gratitude some of the events of this very day.

Next, I invite you to offer thoughts of kindness and goodwill to people in your life. For this exercise you don't need to seek out challenging people - that is another day's work - but offer gentle thoughts to the people you like or love and people who love or like you

A WAVE OF BLESSING AND OTHER MEDITATIONS

Allow yourself a little time for that contemplation.

In conclusion a blessing for you:

> *May you be filled with gratitude as this day comes to a close.*
>
> *May the gift of blessing that you offer to others be its reward for you.*
>
> *May you be satisfied with the work of this day.*
>
> *May you accept the fact that you have done your best in the circumstances.*
>
> *In times of worry may you find comfort in the knowledge that "everything changes."*
>
> *May you rest well.*
>
> *May the gift of rest and sleep enable you to begin again tomorrow with renewed strength.*
>
> *May your days and your nights be filled with peace.*

> "Whatever words we utter should be chosen with care for people will hear them and be influenced by them for good or ill."

Words of the Buddha

4 - A SHORT LITANY OF THANKFULNESS

A couple of days ago I visited a friend. As we sat and chatted in the shade, I couldn't help but notice her dog resting at her feet, the picture of relaxation and contentment. The dog was lying on its side; its legs outstretched, its mouth and nose lying comfortably on the ground. Every so often the dog would give a contented stretch before yawning and relaxing again.

I am not suggesting that to benefit from this reflection you need to lie with your face and nose to the floor but you might like to take a lesson from that little incident and see if you can just sit contentedly for a while and *just be*.

John Milton offers this opening thought:

> *"Gratitude bestows reverence, allowing us to encounter everyday epiphanies, those transcendent moments of awe that change forever how we experience life and the world."*

TONY BRADY

So:

I give thanks for the gift of this new day.

I give thanks for the gift of my life, for my father and mother, my grandparents, great grandparents and ancestors stretching back through the mists of time.

Through some incomprehensible sequence of events, I have come to be here.

That awareness gives me a feeling that my existence is an astonishing gift the response to which must be a continuous *thank you*.

Meister Eckhart tells us that if the only prayer we ever say is *"thank you"* it is enough.

I give thanks for the numberless people who support my life.

I gave thanks for the providers of food, and for the systems that allow me to have light at the tripping of a switch and water at the turn of a tap.

I give thanks for the air I breathe, and for the delicately balanced miracle by which plants give off life-giving oxygen in exchange for the carbon dioxide that we exhale.

A WAVE OF BLESSING AND OTHER MEDITATIONS

I give thanks for the beauty of the earth, for its ever-changing skies, its mountains, hills and valleys, its rivers and lakes and it's interconnected seas washing up on every shore.

I give thanks for the sun that provides us with light and warmth by day and for the magic of the night sky, the moon and the stars, the galaxies made familiar to us through the astounding advances of science.

I give thanks for human intelligence, for our ability to communicate, for the variety of languages and cultures, for the networks of co-operation that enable people to work together for the common good. Let us hope and pray that through becoming more aware of our common humanity we may, at last, learn to use our vast resources for works of peace and let us study war no more.

I give thanks for inspirational leaders and imaginative thinkers, and for all the people throughout history who have inspired us, and who inspire us still, and encourage us to be better people than we might otherwise be.

"At times our light goes out and is rekindled by a spark from another person." In this quote, Albert Schweitzer reminds us that each of us has cause to think with sincere gratitude of those who have lighted the flame within us.

TONY BRADY

I give thanks for those who are different from me, who make me re-examine my views, who do not merely accept the status quo but who have the imagination to ask questions and to dream of things that never were and ask *"why not?"*

May the world around us inspire us to think thoughts of awe and wonder and may happiness, peace, harmony and contentment be the reward of every period in our lives when we stop and look around in gratitude.

A closing thought from Elizabeth Gilbert, the author of Eat, Pray, Love:

> *"In the end, though, maybe we must all give up trying to pay back the people in this world who sustain our lives.*
>
> *In the end, maybe it's wiser to surrender before the miraculous scope of human generosity and just to keep saying thank you, forever and sincerely, for as long as we have voices."*

5 - MEMORIES OF HAPPINESS

As a preliminary to this reflection, I would like you to take a moment or two to become aware of your breath.

You might let to take a deep breath in, hold it for a few seconds and then release it.

You might like to repeat this a couple more times.

When your breathing returns to normal, you might notice how shallowly we usually breathe. Our lungs are hardly expanding at all.

It must help if we can, now and then, become more aware of the breath. As we let a deep breath out, can we in that moment allow our worries and concerns go out with our breath?

We let out a deep sigh as we take a few minutes to step back from the relentless activities of the day.

TONY BRADY

A quote from Khalil Gibran:

> *"If in the twilight of memory we should meet once more, we shall speak again together, and you shall sing to me a deeper song."*

So now I invite you to look back in gratitude at one or two events of your past, some occasions when you were on the receiving end of goodness or kindness.

Take just one minute to see what you can recall.

Did you notice how good it felt to think back on that happy event? It may have happened years ago, even perhaps decades ago, but through the power of recollection, you can bathe in the warm waters of memory.

Sit now for another thirty seconds in that afterglow and enjoy it.

Now can you look back from another angle? On some occasions in the past, you performed some acts of unexpected kindness. We are not looking here for life-changing events, just some occasion when you came to the aid of someone, you were there, and you responded at a moment of need.

A WAVE OF BLESSING AND OTHER MEDITATIONS

Take a minute to look back and see what you find.

How did it feel to remember that good deed? I would say it felt almost as good today as it did on the day you performed it. Someone somewhere is in a better position because of you. The power of good deeds lives on.

So never underestimate your power to do good. You will have seen stones thrown into a calm lake. You will have noticed the ripples. You will have seen ducks paddling across the water, and you will have noticed the V-shaped trail that they leave.

Just like ducks in the water, your actions and mine leave trails in the ocean of life. In fact, all we say and do causes some ripple to move outwards as we journey along. Therefore, every day as we set out in another section on this journey of life let each of us make sure we drop a stone of goodness or give a timely kick and create a stream of goodwill that will radiate out and reach someone who needs some encouragement along the way.

Meditation is a beneficial habit, especially if we can settle down to practice a little every day. Meditation in the morning is an excellent start to any day. It can help make us relaxed and focused. But an essential part of it is the effect that our quiet moments have upon the everyday part of our lives as we go out and about.

TONY BRADY

Meditation isn't just a comfort blanket or a resting cushion. It should prompt us to participate in a life of mindful engagement so that this world will be just a little brighter, a little warmer a little more gentle, because one fateful day we appeared in it.

If at the end of the day, even one life has been made more comfortable because of an encounter with us then our lives will not have been in vain.

Some words of blessing

> *May the blessing of light be upon you,*
>
> *Light on the outside,*
>
> *Light on the inside.*
>
> *With sunlight shining on you,*
>
> *May your heart glow with warmth,*
>
> *Like a fire that welcomes friends and strangers alike.*
>
> *May the light shine from your eyes,*
>
> *Like a candle in the window,*
>
> *Welcoming the weary traveller.*

6 - A BLESSING FOR YOU

We associate the idea of blessing with a priestly caste but John O'Donohue the Irish poet-priest reminds us that we each have the capacity to impart a blessing.

Inspired by the above thought, I invite you to receive this blessing:

I encourage you to prepare by entering your quiet space, sit in your familiar chair, or take up position on your meditation cushion.

Take a few moments to become present, to notice your surroundings, your body, its aches or pains - hopefully and thankfully - the lack of them. Notice your breathing. Put your hand on your chest and feel your heartbeat, listen to the sounds around you, notice the colours of day or the quiet, restful darkness of evening.

I am grateful for my existence in this present moment.

I am grateful for all the benefits of my life.

TONY BRADY

When you are ready, begin to receive this blessing.

Imagine hands being placed on your head or on your shoulders.

Imagine the warmth and comfort of that gentle touch.

Today may loving kindness fill your heart.

Today may you experience acts of loving kindness.

Today may loving kindness be your gift to all the people you meet.

May you never be discouraged by the failures and shortcomings of others.

May those failures act as a stop sign, a warning of what can go wrong when we fall from the narrow path. There but for fortune….

May the failures of others inspire you to do better.

All of us are put to loss by the failure of one, just as all profit by the excellence of one.

Margaret Mead tells us "*Never doubt that a small group of thoughtful, committed citizens can change the world; indeed, it's the only thing that ever has.*"

So, may you be motivated to do good.

And may you be a motivator of others.

May you be aware of the blessings which come to you every day, often without any effort on your part. The love of others, the services of others, the supply of food, water, sanitation, all the benefits of society and not to mention the unnoticed benefits of air, sunlight, the amazing body we each inhabit and this beautiful world in which we all exist.

May your religion, if any, be a religion which inspires you to love and which looks with loving kindness on people who follow a path different to your own.

Is it not wonderful that we are not all the same?

May you be inspired to acts of kindness.

May your acts of kindness be an inspiration to others.

Today, above all, may you be happy and may you radiate happiness wherever you may go.

May you be blessed.

May your life and your light be an inspiration in the world.

Words from the Native American Tradition

"When you arise in the morning, give
thanks for the morning light,
For your life and strength."

7 - AWAKE THE DAWN

Welcome to this morning reflection as we awake to the light of a new day.

As we begin, I invite you to take a deep breath and draw your attention to the most incredible fact that you can imagine. The fact that *you* are alive here and now.

And, amazingly, we are not really generally aware of this gift.

Through the miracle of print, you are reading this.

You might be around the corner from me here in Dublin or you might sitting halfway across the planet, this oasis of life, a fragile blue ball spinning and hurtling through space at speed beyond imagining as you sit in your meditation space oblivious to the fact that we are moving at all.

But incredible as all this is you can somehow get your head around it. After all the planet changed over aeons of time, and eventually people evolved on the earth to the point where they could create the language, the printed characters and finally the book that is in your hand.

But your individual existence is genuinely amazing beyond your wildest imaginings. The fact that you and I are here at all is just beyond extraordinary considering that each of us is the product of countless possibilities, and numberless combinations of co-incidences required to happen over millennia to result in you and I being here today.

So as we awake to the light of a new day the first thought which must come to our minds must be one of profound gratitude. We have done nothing to deserve what is indeed a gift beyond price.

A pause might be appropriate to allow ourselves a moment to express thanks for the astonishing fact of our existence.

A quote from John O'Donohue:

> *"Each morning, we awaken to the light and the invitation to a new day in the world of time."*

Now that we are here on this extraordinary journey the question is *how can we possibly respond to it?* If we had won the lotto there would be the more straightforward question of whether we should spend the money on ourselves or put it to use where it is needed most.

But this life of ours is even more finite and more precious than money, and the limited time of our life is ours to apply in the way *we* decide.

So today resolve to make a small difference in *your* world. For most of us, it is a little world, our neighbourhood, the place where we work and play, and of course our own home and our family circle. Some readers of this might have the privilege and responsibility of influencing people on a broader scale and, if you are one of them, may all our blessings accompany you in that endeavour. The commitment to good where someone is in a position of influence is a real gift in response to which a person would be happy to dedicate a whole life's work.

But in the ordinary life of every one of us, there is a space where our talents and our opportunities overlap and here is where we can make a difference in our little world. It begins when we encounter the very first person we meet in the day. It can be someone at home or someone near us, someone whom possibly we take for granted. Can we remember today to look on that first person with eyes of real compassion and interest?
As the day proceeds can we watch out for opportunities to do good, to offer the encouraging word, to volunteer to help, to carefully listen and to listen without feeling the need to step in with an early reply? Sometimes all the other person requires is that we be there, paying attention. And you will be surprised when you observe how rare it is

for people to actually attend to what others are saying. It is as if we are 90% broadcasters and only 10% receivers.

So let us give ourselves a moment to consider the people and the circumstance we are likely to encounter today and see if we can plan to be the light in someone else's life before this day ends.

There are many opportunities for involved social action, and we might see if we can manage to dedicate time in an organised way to help lubricate the wheels of society. If we were to suffer the loss of the voluntary sector the world would be a much more miserable place, not only for those who are worked for but for those who themselves benefit from the built-in reward that comes from helping others.

Even a few hours a week can make a difference, and if you become involved in a group, it will lessen the opportunity of putting off the good deed or postponing the good intention until some "more convenient time." Some people require help with literacy including computer literacy. People living alone may need someone to visit.

Every place will have organisations who will be pleased to accept new volunteers so if you can manage to do so you might consider lending a hand by freely offering other people some of the time of your life.

A WAVE OF BLESSING AND OTHER MEDITATIONS

As the well-known hymn by Carol Owens says *"Freely, freely you have received, freely, freely give."*

But it is in the everyday encounters that we can make the most significant difference. We can achieve this by watching out for the other. We can deliberately make the first approach, making an opportunity to speak to someone who appears alone or distressed. We must simply watch out for, and listen to, the people we meet day by day and not take other people for granted.

Today is an incredible new day. It is really beyond belief that we are here. The least we can do is to respond with gratitude expressed in love and concern for our fellow travellers on this remarkable journey of life.

So today let us put our best foot forward and act as people of peace. Hopefully, we will not encounter hatred but where we do let us not add fuel to that fire.

Let us see difference as something to be celebrated and not feared,

Let gloom act our prompt to turn on a little light.

If we see someone bereaved, let us realise that we cannot understand how they feel. So just be with the bereaved person.

If we encounter sadness, let ours be the listening ear, someone who shows a willingness to listen and who tries to understand.

If someone points to a glass half empty, always draw attention to the fact that the glass is also half full.

If we see someone in despair let us try to find some reason for hope, however slight.

In a world where truth is harder to find let us do nothing to spread rumours. Before we speak let our word pass through these three gates:

Is it true?

Is it necessary?

Is it kind?

Observe that in the depths of the best of us there is the frightening capacity to do wrong so remember to water and nurture the seeds of goodness in ourselves and others.

Realise that in the heart of the worst of us there is some spark of goodness. Try to find that spark and attempt to kindle it further.

8 - GATEWAY TO EMPATHY

This next meditation will, I hope, will help us place ourselves in the shoes of another person. We will try to feel how they feel, imagine what they desire, try to experience their fears, picture their loneliness, share their dreams.

Extending empathy is like giving someone a psychological hug, and that is what we are going to try to practice in this reflection.

So begin by setting down into that most elusive of states, quietness, the task of meeting our daily challenge to slow down, stop for a moment and *just be*.

You might begin by taking a few deep breaths, remembering that inhalation and exhalation are doorways to awareness of this present moment.

Take a deep breath in, hold, then let it completely out.

Repeat this a couple of times.

Now totally relax, let your breathing return to normal and, on each exhalation, think of the word *"relax."*

Realise that all is well in this time and place.

All is well in the here and the now.

A thought from Daniel H Pink:

> *"Empathy is about standing in someone else's shoes, feeling with his or her heart, seeing with his or her eyes. it makes the world a better place."*

Continue by calling to mind someone you know, at this point think not of someone who is specially close to you, but someone with whom you have a reasonably comfortable relationship.

H Jackson Brown tells us *"Remember that everyone you meet is afraid of something, loves something and has lost something."*

A WAVE OF BLESSING AND OTHER MEDITATIONS

So just picture the selected person in your mind's eye and hold them in your thoughts for a moment of attentive reflection.

Still keeping that person in mind try now to imagine how they might be feeling today. Think about how they might have begun their day, alone or with others, how they might have thought as they faced into the day. Did they go to work? Are they studying? perhaps looking after a family at home, maybe this is someone who has recently been made redundant or unemployed, possibly having moved house, or needing to move house, perhaps having lately married or having lost a partner.

Bearing in mind as John Cunningham says *"Empathy is full presence to what's alive in the other person at this moment."* please give yourself a little time to stand in that person's shoes as they are today.

Next look back and see if you can imagine that person's childhood, their growing up, getting through adolescence, finding their way in the world, their challenges, ambitions, hopes, struggles.

Another pause as you reflect with compassion on the circumstances that might have combined to make that person the individual they are today.

Dietrich Bonhoeffer tells us that we must learn to regard people less in the light of what they do or omit to do, and more in the light of what they suffer.

So next consider how that person might be facing the future. How they might be coping with older age, the loss of a partner or perhaps never having had an intimate companion. What about financial worries, how might that individual be looking to future events, who do they call, whom could they call if in trouble? Could the person concerned appreciate the fact that they could call on you in a moment of difficulty?

A final pause while you hold that person in your mind and heart in a spirit of empathy.

What we have been attempting here is referred to in Buddhism as *Karuna*. Karuna means having active sympathy or a willingness to bear the pain of others.

You can apply this exercise to the people you know. You can practice it on your nearest (but still never entirely understood) dearest, and extend your compassion out to other people and then even out to people with whom you have a problematic relationship.

When we meditate we try to quieten our minds, we attempt to come into the present; we resolve to approach the day in a spirit of calm, we try to be less subject to the winds that blow us the direction of annoyance or revenge or anything of that sort.

A WAVE OF BLESSING AND OTHER MEDITATIONS

This effort to direct our intentions in a right way, or as it is called *a skillful direction*, is an agreeable and helpful way to approach the days of our lives.

If we work at this, we will have no regrets when we come to look back over our years. Our lives can be a blessing to others, but this benediction is an accumulation of kindnesses practiced over time, day by day, hour by hour.

It will help us in these efforts if we can try to form the habit of putting ourselves in the shoes of the other.

As Henry David Thoreau puts it *"Could a greater miracle take place than for us to look through each other's eyes for an instant?"*

The Native American Cherokee tribe have a saying *"Don't judge a man until you have walked a mile in his shoes."*

Underneath their surface differences, every person we meet, the friendly, the unfriendly, the aloof, the troublesome and all in between share the hopes, dreams and fears that are common to all humanity. Each and every one got up this morning to face a new day. Everyone seeks happiness. Each person wishes to love and be loved. Every individual will fear pain and loneliness. Each one of us needs a listening ear. All of us will benefit from empathy, and every one of us can supply that gift of understanding or Karuna.

TONY BRADY

As Stephen Covey reminds us *"To touch the soul of another human being is to walk on holy ground."*

A practice we might attempt as we go about the business of the day would be to try to remember to look on everyone we meet with eyes of compassion. Try to see through the sometimes brash confidence, the annoying arrogance, the frightening intolerance, to the vulnerable oversized child within and see if we can manage to offer that person a silent blessing.

May you be well,

May you be happy,

May you be healthy,

May you be free from suffering.

And that is my wish for you too as we come to the end of this reflection.

May YOU be well,
may YOU be happy,
may YOU be healthy,
may YOU be free from suffering,

And in reviewing the events of your life may you recognise that all your unspoken dreams have in fact come true.

9 - SUPPORT IN A TIME OF BEREAVEMENT

We may be fortunate enough not to suffer the loss of a loved one for many years, but sooner or later the pain of bereavement affects every one of us.

Welcome to this reflection which is designed to offer you support on the loss of a loved one. You and I know that little that anyone can say can guarantee to offer you comfort at a time like this.

No one feels your pain precisely just now.

But the thought that others are reading this, themselves seeking support in a time of loss, may be a comfort to you in knowing that you are not alone.

Helen Keller tells us *"We bereaved are not alone. We belong to the largest company in all the world—the company of those who have known suffering."*

So, we begin by recognising that we support one another in this time of anguish. We are here for one another as we reflect on the loss of someone we have loved.

We don't suggest that *time will heal* or that *you must get over it*. We pray that the passage of time will bring some healing, but we recognise that the loss of someone dear to us is a real and permanent loss.

Love is priceless, its currency is remembrance, and the currency of remembrance never loses value. It takes time. But for sure and finally, time will come to help us as we pick up the pieces knowing that even though love is forever, life must go on. But healing takes time.

So let us begin by seeing if we can be present for some other bereaved person in this shared circumstance which we have long put to the back of our minds. This is a day that we had hoped would never come to pass.

Give yourself a time for silent reflection where it is alright to shed a tear, and it is useful to know that in doing so you are not on your own.

Remember and take comfort from the fact that other people reading this will understand what it is to suffer a bereavement. You are not alone.

A WAVE OF BLESSING AND OTHER MEDITATIONS

A quote from – Washington Irving:

> *"There is a sacredness in tears. They are not the mark of weakness, but of power. They speak more eloquently than ten thousand tongues. They are messengers of overwhelming grief and unspeakable love."*

In our longest days and our darkest nights we will remember you.

The loss of a life partner, perhaps someone to whom you have spoken the words *"till death us do part"* or *"so long as we both shall live"* is one example of the anguish we experience when a loved one dies.

There is the tragic premature death of a child, something parents never expect will happen. It is natural, even though painful, to see our parents die, but who expects to experience the heartbreak of losing a child?

There are babies born who bring joy to their parents for only the briefest of moments. We need to call to mind the fact that each new life no matter how fragile or short forever changes the world. "*I held you every second of your life."*
- Stephanie Paige Cole

There is the loss of siblings, the loss of neighbours, the loss of friends. One associate of mine who lost a friend was offered the advice *"But Mary you have lots of other friends."* A distraught Mary responded by protesting *"Yes, I have other friends, but I am sad because I have lost this one."* Each one of us is unique, special, irreplaceable.

Then there are the different circumstances surrounding death, death by accident, death through illness, death through violence, death in time of war. There is the tragedy of suicide when someone in distress decides that life is no longer worth living. If only they had spoken to someone. Everyone, anyone, would have been glad to offer support and hope. Suicide is such a tragic, such a painful loss. We keep asking *"If only?"*

The singer songwriter Mick Hanley captures some of our emotions perfectly in his song *"I feel should be calling you."* We have all experienced that feeling. Mick Hanley's lyrics include the lines:

> *"Sometimes the telephone is in my hand*
> *Then I realise anew that there's*
> *no-one there at all,*
> *No footstep in the hall*
> *It's a silence that's so hard to*
> *understand."*

A WAVE OF BLESSING AND OTHER MEDITATIONS

In all this we see that the most prolonged life is so short, no matter how long, life is always *"done too soon"* as far as the companionship of our loved ones is concerned.

Cicero tells us that the life given us by nature is short, but the memory of a life well spent is eternal.

Let's pause for a couple of minutes to think of others who are reading this reflection and let us dedicate this time of reflection to them. May every reading of this meditation be a reassurance to them and a reminder to us that the bereaved are not alone.

In our longest days and our darkest nights, we will remember you.

Different religions and philosophies offer differing ideas as to what might follow after we die and this can provide much comfort and support depending upon one's beliefs. For myself, I find it hard to believe that this is it, that there is no meaning beyond this wondrous journey onto which we have all set sail.

Nevertheless, in this reflection and to make it relevant to everyone regardless of belief or unbelief, we will leave thoughts of a world to come to one side and concentrate on what all of us, irrespective of our differing creeds and views, can see and know for sure.

In feeling pain at the fact that someone has died, it might be helpful to reflect with gratitude on the astonishing fact that they lived at all. We reflect on the wonder and that we came to know and to love them and that they came to know and love us. There is the Hebrew proverb: "*Say not in grief 'he is no more' but in thankfulness that he was.*"

Often we can gain some comfort by taking up the good work to which our friend may have dedicated much of his or her life.

I have been unable to ascertain the name of the author of this quote to the same effect:

> "*As long as I can I will look at this world for both of us, as long as I can, I will sing with the birds, I will laugh with the flowers, I will pray to the stars, for both of us.*"

Frequently we feel we did not express love to the other in the way that we should. It is better not to dwell on that omission. It is a typical enough experience where we repeat in our minds the words *"If only."* But we can take comfort from the fact that our loved ones, if we could ask them, would very likely feel the very same about us.

If we have any feelings of lingering regret, let us make amends by giving the care to others that we believe we should have given to our deceased friend. Above all let this reflection be a reminder that we should listen more to others, watch out more for others, be present more for others. Life is short, and we are all fellow travellers on the extraordinary journey that is our life together.

At this stage I suggest a pause for a minute to see how you might make up in the future for any neglect you might feel in respect of the past. Let this time of loss be a new beginning.

Regardless of the past, you can begin again. *"Starting over is an acceptance of a past we can't change, an unrelenting conviction that the future can be different, and the stubborn wisdom to use the past to make the future what the past was not."* - Craig D. Lounsbrough.

"I still miss those I loved who are no longer with me, but I find I am grateful for having loved them. The gratitude has finally conquered the loss." - Rita Mae Brown.

I would like end this reflection by sharing with you a meditation which I wrote following the death of a friend of mine. In the same way, you might find it helpful to write down your thoughts about some person whom you have loved and lost.

TONY BRADY

This reflection is called *"My Friend Paul."*

My friend Paul was a man who loved to spend time in meditation. It was appropriate that he should come to spend his last minutes of life in the very hour when I was listening to a reflection on the theme of *transience*.

The mindfulness teacher to whom I was listening suggested that it would be a good idea to dedicate the sitting for the benefit of someone who was facing change, or death - as indeed Paul was - and so I did.

Then as I ended the meditation and checked my phone, I saw a message to the effect that, a little while earlier, Paul, as it was put *"had gone to live with the angels."*

His timing was just about perfect. The death of someone we know and love gives rise to questions which have been asked by people since the dawn of time. *"What is life all about?" "How did I come to be here?", "Where do we come from?" "Do we go somewhere else when this life is over?"* and of course for finite beings in a vast cosmos, there is no absolute answer.

But the Buddhist monk and peace activist Thich Nhat Hanh, whom Paul and I much admire, denies that something can come into being from nothing. For something like that to happen just does not make any sense. Neither can something already existing go out of existence, even though its form may change.

And how is it that, surrounded as we are by death and change, none of us can imagine or believe in our non-existence? Thoughts along these lines lead me to conclude that, in some incomprehensible manner, we do in fact go on and that there is much more to the reality of our being than meets the eye.

I'm sure that in any future life, many people would not particularly wish to see me again, but I imagine my friend Paul might like to bump into me. He was one of the kindest, most reliable, trustworthy people I ever had the good fortune to meet. He was devoted to his wife Ann whom he loved with all his heart. We made some trips to places of meditation, Plum Village near Bordeaux in France, Jampa Ling in Cavan in Ireland. Always there was the daily report back to Ann to enquire if she was well. The words *"I love you"* were repeated with sincerity in all those conversations. I recall fearing one time that we might never make it safely back to Dublin, Paul driving at an over anxious speed, back to the arms of his beloved.

Paul idolised his children. He greatly missed Michael, a son whom he had lost a little while before I met him. His children were all "the greatest" in his eyes. He thought I was great too, but that didn't give me a swelled head because Paul gave everyone the benefit of the doubt. In his world, the glass was always half full, if not filled to overflowing. He had the best doctor, the best hospital, the best advisors, the best friends. It seems that being the best himself, he was rewarded with, and attracted the companionship of, people who shared his positive attitude to life. They say that that has something to do with Karma.

Paul's good, decent, caring life reminds me that we are all here for only a short time, even those of us who manage to hang in long beyond our sell-by date.

But the life of each of us is a gift beyond price, inexplicable, incredible, unearned, undeserved. So each of us must try to make the best use of this benefit. My friend Paul never preached about doing good; he just practiced it to the end.

And so the time has come to say goodbye. Sleep well my friend; I hope, I feel sure, we will meet again sometime, we will catch up on the news and explore with even more amazement an even vaster world. When? Does it matter? As Thich Nhat Hahn would remind us, we have forever, and forever is a long, long time.

10 - A KEY TO HAPPINESS

I invite you to sit for a while in meditation at the end of this chapter to ask yourself if you can put any of this into effect.

Wouldn't it be wonderful if we could all be happy?

But how can I be happy if you are not happy and if I know I am to blame for your unhappiness?

There is an expression in the Irish language for a self-obsessed individual- the words are "Mé Féin" two words which mean *"myself."*

Mé Féin-ism as we call it, is an expression used to express disapproval of a selfish person. We deride the attitude of such an individual as being in the *"I'm alright Jack"* category, an attitude summarised in the expression *"everyone for himself"*

It is an attitude which has traditionally been despised and for excellent reason.

We are not a community broken down into individuals although Margaret Thatcher once, rather unfortunately, said, *"there is no such thing as society."* The sentence continued *"there are individual men and women, and there are families."*

What the stateswoman appeared to be trying to get across at the time was the need for people who could do so, to get doing things for themselves, rather than sitting back and expecting society to provide for individuals who were themselves well capable of contributing to the community.

But uttering the words, *"there is no such thing as society"* was missing the reality. There is a society, and each of us is an individual living in and supporting one another in that society. We are not independent individuals, each one paddling his or her own canoe. We are all part of an interdependent web of all existence. John Greenleaf Whittier describes this interdependence in his famous quote *"Pluck one thread, and the web ye mar, break but one of a thousand keys and the paining jar through all will run".*

There is an unfortunate modern tendency to talk about the importance of looking after yourself first. People say *"You must look after number one."*

Despite the quote, I do not think that those expressing the *"no society"* view are, on their own, to blame for our current malaise. Our selfishness may just have something to do with our built-in primitive animal instinct for survival.

But having gone beyond that purely base animal stage, we have to bring back to mind our societal obligations to the people around us. In the Bible Jesus tells us to *"love your neighbour as yourself."*

There is regrettably little sharing in the prosperous part of the world. It is a society where more and more people each have their individual rooms, their own TV sets, their personal music systems, their personal computers, their private phones. This affluent world is also a place where there is, it appears, more and more unhappiness.

In our material prosperity, we have not only put ourselves first but kept ourselves preeminent. As a result, we have more and more of what we here in Ireland refer to as Mé Féin-ism. We have each become our own be-all and end-all and the resultant feeling is not good. It has not led to an increase in contentment. In fact the opposite is the case.

Admittedly if we are on a flight and the air pressure suddenly falls and we see the oxygen masks presented, we realise we must put on our protection first or we will be unable to do anything for ourselves or the people around us. But having put on our life saving device, we must then attend to the needs of the people next to us.

We would not, I hope, sit back and think it better to leave others unattended so that we might have more oxygen for ourselves. That would be a shameful act of selfishness of which hardly any of us would approve. So, in our hearts we know that we should support one another.

Our altruism comes to the fore when there is an emergency. One person jumps without hesitation into the sea to rescue another; someone else runs into a burning building to save someone in danger. Our instinct in an emergency is to come to the aid of someone in need.

But in our prosperity, we can become blind to the needs of others, believing everyone will be quite alright on their own. Of course, the plain fact is that they are not alright.

There are some keys to finding happiness in life. One such key arises from having a sense of gratitude. Just look around and consider all the reasons we have for thankfulness. The practice of gratitude is a subject worthy of regular reflective meditation in its own right.

And on a daily basis, we will find it to be the case that happiness always comes from happiness shared.

The problem is that when the going is easy, we drift back into the complacency of looking after ourselves first *and* last. Our very prosperity can lead to our downfall.

Happiness will not endure by keeping it to one's self.

So, next time someone tells you to look after yourself first, remember to enquire directly and firmly *"and then what?"*

11 - MEDITATION TECHNIQUES

To bring yourself into the present moment you can try any technique that works for you. Here are some suggestions:

1. You might find it helpful is to close your eyes and concentrate on a spot which you imagine to be in the distance beyond the tip of your nose - just focus on that place and ignore anything else that floats across your mind.

2. An idea you might like to try comes from the fact that we can only think of one thing at a time. So why not try counting from one to seven and back slowly and repeatedly on your in breath or outbreath. When you get to seven count down again to one and so on. If you lose count, just start again at number one.

3. During your meditation time, you might like to concentrate on just one person whom you love or whom you have loved. Hold that person in your heart, imagine their face and let everything else just be.

4. You might prefer to concentrate on some object in your meditation space. The item might be a candle, a flower, perhaps an image of the Buddha or Jesus or some other inspirational person and just be with that figure or object.

5. Why not recall some beautiful place which you have visited and relax in the warm feeling that comes from having been there?

6. You could decide to focus on your breath, breathing in and being aware that you are breathing in, breathing out and being aware that you are breathing out. As you do this, try not to control the speed of your breath. Just breathe naturally. If your mind wanders, and you may expect that it will, don't let that worry you, just bring your focus back to your breath.

7. You might sound a bell and as it fades, notice the sound fading into the distance and imagine the sound still fading further as it becomes less and less.

8. Why not try to do a body scan starting with your feet and moving slowly up to your head. The idea is that you flex and un-flex each body part in turn. This action helps you to become aware of the gift that is your body.

9. Perhaps turn your attention to how the body moves as you inhale and exhale. Notice your chest and belly expanding and contracting as you breath in and out.

10. You might lie to repeat a manta or a prayer. It can be a traditional prayer or something as simple as *"may peace prevail on earth"* or *"my existence is a miracle"* or something that you have come across in a book or online.

11. You could use either the simple *"Aum"*, *"Om"*: which is considered to be the vibration of universal consciousness. It is a sound used in Buddhism and other traditions. You don't have to say it aloud.

You can experiment with these and other techniques all designed to help you with your practice of concentration.

And in all this try to remember that the practice of meditation or mindfulness is a means to an end, not an end in itself. Enjoy the journey and stick with the practice.

It will have been a worthwhile effort if meditation and reflection leads you to a position where your everyday actions make a difference in the world around you.

To enjoy good health,
to bring true happiness to
one's family, to bring peace
to all, one must first
discipline and control one's
own mind. If a man can
control his mind he can find
the way to Enlightenment,
and all wisdom and virtue
will naturally come
to him.

Words of the Buddha

12 - SLOWING AND STOPPING

When did you last slow down, really slow down?

When did you last stop, really stop?

Eddie Cantor tells us "*Slow down and enjoy life. It's not only the scenery you miss by going too fast - you also miss the sense of where you are going and why.*"

Welcome to this reflection on slowing and stopping

We live in an increasingly frenetic world. A world where we seem to be addicted to ever increasing speed.

But just observe the motions of nature. We see that the earth revolves at a steady pace. The moon revolves around our planet every four weeks. The earth completes its 940 million kilometres (584 million miles) journey around the sun every year. We have no awareness of this movement because it is so steady, so reliable.

If the earth were to suddenly spin more quickly we would be momentarily swept off our feet, but we need have no fear of that because in the world of nature it is almost always a case of *"steady as she goes."*

You might like to pause, notice and be grateful for the all the things around you that are stable and consistent.

But in the human world, it is a different matter. Here we seek quicker results, faster trains, bigger planes, immediate cures, prompt pain-relief, instant coffee, ready-made meals, fast food consumed on the go as we instantaneously communicate with people near and far on our new devices.

And of course, just as soon as (or before) we become reasonably familiar with our current tech-tools a still-newer more modern better version is advertised in our world which is engaged in a frenzy of built-in obsolescence. In this fast-paced environment, even our attention spans are falling. This has reached a the point where programme makers have to increase the speed of scene changes before we rapidly lose interest in whatever they wish to show us.

There is a feeling that unless we move very quickly, we are not keeping up, we are not efficient. Which of us will happily we feel comfortable admitting that we are not busy? Aren't we all expected to be run off our feet? Do we not use this constant busyness to justify our existence?

A WAVE OF BLESSING AND OTHER MEDITATIONS

There is no need to speed up the recorded images of a busy railway, airport or underground station. Life as we live it is revealed to be fast enough even if played back at its original speed.

A quote - (author unknown)

Please slow me down; I'm rushing here and there

Rushing down my meals, dashing everywhere

Queuing in the Post Office, I cannot wait in line

Trotting out again, to come another time.

Shift me to a lower gear and give me time to chat,

To see a baby in a pram, or a dog that needs a pat

Help me to look upward and admire the towering trees

*Remind me there is more to life
than all this foolish speed.*

Help me to admire the hills and the eternal streams

Let me, in my hours of sleep, appreciate my dreams

Why not pause now to recall the speed at which you do

things while also thinking of the next item on your list.

This exhortation to slow down is one which I have to repeat not only to people who are reading this book but to myself also.

I recall that when I first started uploading meditations to the Insight Timer App, many people helpfully reminded me that I needed to slow down my speed of speaking. That hurried pace was something of which I was completely unaware until it was pointed out to me.

Even now, and so many meditations later, there is the occasional comment *"I wish he had spoken more slowly."* Once I recall someone commenting *"He urges us to slow down, but he speaks so fast himself."* This is something that I must constantly remind myself when speaking in public. This reminder to myself is aided by a note on the top of each printed page in large font "SLOW DOWN."

The problem I think, is that some of us have the tendency to speak as quickly as we read and that pace is not at all helpful in our effort to communicate with others. And of course, if we are anxious, we tend to speak even more quickly than we would if we were in a more relaxed state.

But we have to remember that by speaking too fast we are adding to the general feeling of urgency in the world and we are giving people around us the impression that there is not enough time in which to get things done. This feeling of being rushed is a sensation most people already have in abundance, and they do not desire any more of it.

When listening to someone who is speaking loudly, it will help quieten the tone of the conversation if you can remember to talk back in a whisper. If you speak quietly you may expect the other person will be less likely to shout

We might now pause for reflection, just for a few moments, to consider our own speaking pace and think about how, by slowing down our own speed of speech we might encourage a greater sense of calm among the people around us.

So in the days ahead see if you can go more slowly and more mindfully about your life.

Try this experiment:
Read any sentence at a fast pace. Then read the same sentence but this time very slowly. Notice how time seems to stretch when you read more slowly. Notice how the *"now"* of the reading expands.

People frequently make comments to the effect that every year which passes seems faster than the one which went before. This certainly appears to be the case. There are many theories as to why this might seem to be so. One notion is that a year just past is a more significant percentage of the life-to-date of a young person. A year to a child of seven is one-seventh of the child's entire life. A year in my life is one-seventieth of what has gone before. Is it any wonder then, that for me, time appears to fly?

Another possibility may be that we compress the *"now"* by moving or speaking at a faster rate. So, try in the days and weeks ahead, to see if you can make the present moment last longer by slowing down the speed of your speech and by deliberately slowing down the pace of your activity.

To help you in this here is a well-known reflection from Wilfred A. Peterson:

> *Slow me down Lord*
> *Ease the pounding of my heart*
> *by the quieting of my mind.*
>
> *Steady my hurried pace*
> *with a vision of the eternal march of time.*
>
> *Give me amid the confusion of the day,*
> *the calmness of the eternal hills.*
>
> *Break the tension of my nerves and*
> *muscles*
> *with the soothing music of the singing*
> *streams*
> *that live in my memory.*

*Help me to know the magical restoring
power of sleep.*

*Teach me the art of taking minute
vacations,*

*Of slowing down to look at a flower,
to chat with a friend,
to pat a dog,
to read a few lines of a good book.*

*Slow me down Lord
and inspire me to send my roots
deep into the soil of life's enduring values
that I may grow toward
the stars of my greater destiny.*

TONY BRADY

Words from the Native American Tradition

Oh Great Spirit,
Whose voice I hear in the winds,
And whose breath gives life to all the world,
hear me!
I am small and weak,
I need your strength and wisdom.

Let me walk in beauty, and make my eyes
ever behold the red and purple sunset.

Make my hands respect the things you have made
and my ears sharp to hear your voice.

Make me wise so that I may understand the
things you have taught my people.

Let me learn the lessons you have hidden
in every leaf and rock.

I seek strength, not to be greater than my brother,
but to fight my greatest enemy – myself.

Make me always ready to come to you with
clean hands and straight eyes.

So when life fades, as the fading sunset
my spirit may come to you without shame.

13 - WE ARE BLESSED TODAY

Each of us woke up today to the magic that is the unearned gift of our existence.

Our circumstances vary.

We are female and male, and some are in between.

Old and young, and some are in between.

We are rich and poor, and some are in between.

Some are black, some white, and some are in between.

In some extraordinary way, all of us, are at this stopping place, a momentary pause on a journey between the wonder of birth and the mystery of death.

Today, just now at this moment, we are all one in experiencing the marvel, the amazement that is our life.

TONY BRADY

Our lives and circumstances, whatever they may be, represent a blessing beyond imagining.

This quote comes from the Buddha:

> *"If we could see the miracle*
> *of a single flower clearly,*
> *our whole life would change."*

So:

May we open our eyes to become aware of the gift that is our life.

If we have the gift of sight may we explore the world around us as if we are seeing it for the first, or the last, time.

If we have the gift of hearing, may we listen to the sounds of the world around us, and the voices of the people around us, as if we are experiencing these sounds and the words of our companions for the first, or the last, time.

If we have the gift of smell, may we examine the varied scents of our world as if we had arrived as visitors from another planet.

A WAVE OF BLESSING AND OTHER MEDITATIONS

Just look at the way a baby touches and feels objects placed at its side. Here, without any training is a young life open to, and exploring, its new astounding world. When did we last explore with fascination the different textures of the objects which surround us?

We have launched out into space, and we are rightly thrilled at what our probes are sending back, but we take our home planet for granted. In our mindlessness we have laid waste to the Earth, plundered its finite resources and tuned its oceans into a receptacle for our waste.

There is only one Earth, and there is magic here for us if we can just recapture our lost ability to pay attention.

A quote from Maya Angelou:

> *"The thing to do, it seems to me, is to prepare yourself so you can be a rainbow in somebody else's cloud.*
> *Somebody who may not look like you.*
> *May not call God the same name you call God - if they call God at all.*
> *May not dance your dances or speak your language.*
> *But be a blessing to somebody.*
> *That's what I think."*

So, in light of that quote:

May you be a blessing to everyone you meet today

May you be light in every problematic situation.

May you be a place of refuge in someone's storm.

May you be a comfort in someone's grief, encouragement in someone's hope.

May the world be a little brighter because you have woken up the gift of this new day.

The message of this reflection is that you have received blessings beyond measure, beyond your wildest dreams.

You have, here in your possession, in your very hands, what Mary Oliver describes as this *"wild and precious life"* She asks *what will you do with it?*

We don't have to imagine or worry about a lifetime of good works, though that can be the happy result of what we do day by day.

We just have to resolve to be a light in the world today. That is all we need to do for today.

Let us conclude this reflection with this Irish blessing:

"May you be poor in misfortune,
Rich in blessings,
Slow to make enemies,
Quick to make friends,
But rich or poor, quick or slow,
May you know nothing but happiness
from this day forward."

TONY BRADY

Words from the Native American Tradition

We return thanks to our mother,
the Earth, which sustains us.
We return thanks to the rivers and streams,
which supply us with water.
We return thanks to all herbs,
which furnish medicines for the cure of our diseases.
We return thanks to the moon and stars,
which have given to us their light when the sun was gone.
We return thanks to the sun,
that has looked upon the Earth with a beneficent eye.
Lastly, we return thanks to the Great Spirit,
in whom is embodied all goodness,
and who directs all things for the good of her children.

14 - FOR TODAY, JUST LET THINGS BE

Good morning, or afternoon, or evening as you sit down to read this chapter.

Whoever you are, wherever you are, wherever you are on your journey of life, you are welcome to this reflection.

For next little while, as you read this, you are encouraged just to allow things to be or as the song says *"Let the world turn without you."* See if you can be present in this moment.

If you have a meditation bell, you might like to begin this reflection by sounding an opening bell.

As the sound fades see if you can let your worries dissolve along with the sound of the chime.

Make sure you are comfortable in whatever position suits yourself. This is intended as an endurance test.

Just relax.

Take a deep breath in - we don't usually breathe thoroughly. You might ask how the lower half of our lungs ever get enough oxygen to keep our bodies working.

Hold that breath for a second or two.

Then slowly breathe out.

Again - deep breath in - hold – then a slow breath out.

Once more – a deep breath in - notice your chest and belly expanding - hold – and a slow breath out.

Now let your breathing return to normal.

Simply relax, let things be, we are not trying our clear our minds, we are just paying quiet attention to what is happening, not getting involved as ideas come and go. As you notice these interruptions, just think to yourself *"I will deal with you later."* For now, this is *taking it easy* time.

Next, we carry out a quick check on our bodies, first of all flexing our toes, then our feet, moving up to our calves, then our thighs, next pulling in our abdomen, then tightening our chest, then flexing our upper arms, our forearms, then our hands, moving then to our fingers, contracting our neck, then our face, even our eyes.

Notice all the marvellous working parts of the body. If some parts are not working to perfection be grateful for the parts that are. This is an amazing construction.

Try it again.

Flexing our toes, then our feet, calves, thighs, pulling in our abdomen, tightening our chest, flexing our upper arms, the forearms, then hands, fingers, tightening our neck, our face, our eyes. In each case then letting go.

This exercise helps us be aware of our bodies, working away, day and night. It is a great gift to be alive.

The next part of this exercise is where we just pay attention to the sounds around us, the near sounds, then moving out to the far sounds. In this exercise we are solely paying attention to what is happening in the sound world. Again, if ideas come (as they will), just notice them, tell them you will deal with them later. For now, we are taking in the astonishing world of sound.

As we repeat these exercises, it is important to be gentle with ourselves. No one is checking up on you.

Training the mind has been described as a task like training a puppy. You gently encourage the little animal to sit. The puppy sits for a second or two, then it runs away.

There is no use hitting the puppy or shouting at it. You know that such an approach won't work. You just gently, calmly, repeatedly ask the puppy to sit, again and again.

Then someday the puppy will sit quietly in response to the command. Great, you think the training is complete. Success. You are excited. But the very next day the puppy runs away when you tell it to sit down. Patience needed.

We can be just like that scatter-brained puppy. But do not let this worry you at all. Observing this behaviour tin ourselves tells us a lot about how un-concentrated we can be at times. Meditation is a training in concentration.

Next, you might like to sound the bell again for the end of this reflection. You don't have to resume your activities immediately.

You can take a little more time if you wish.

But as the sound fades, and in the time following, just consider the next 24 hours that lie ahead and resolve to approach that time in a mindful, caring way, a way that will help circulate a little kindness and help make the world a better place.

15 - GRATITUDE FOR A NEW DAY

This next reflection is designed to help you offer thanks for each new day.

Every new day is a gift. We are inclined to feel that we have an endless supply of days, but that is not the case. One day the stock will run out.

So just now give thanks for your life renewed as you awake to the light of another new day and another new beginning

It is helpful to begin any reflection by trying to get yourself into a comfortable position. Find a quiet regular place if you have one, but in any event, attempt to establish a peaceful space within your own head. This is the locality where there is the most noise.

Notice the sounds around you, starting with the near sounds, then noticing more distant sounds.

Notice your breathing – your life-giving breath going in and out.

TONY BRADY

A thought from the Metta Sutta – the Buddha's words on Loving Kindness:

> *"This is what should be done by one who*
> *is skilled in goodness,*
> *and who knows the path of peace:*
>
> *Let them be able and upright,*
> *Straightforward and gentle in speech,*
>
> *Humble and not conceited,*
> *Contented and easily satisfied,*
>
> *Unburdened with duties*
> *and frugal in their ways.*
>
> *Peaceful & calm and wise and skillful,*
> *not proud or demanding in nature.*
>
> *Let them not do the slightest thing that*
> *the wise would later reprove."*

I suggest you might spend 60 seconds, one quiet minute to generate thoughts of gratitude for the gift of your existence in this very day.

If there is a worry troubling you, just sit with it for a while. Recognise this as your current reality. There is no need to bury it. But it will help if you just recall the fact that *everything changes* and this trouble or pain will change too.

A WAVE OF BLESSING AND OTHER MEDITATIONS

Very often our anticipation of trouble causes us more discomfort than the actual difficulty of the moment. Thankfully *everything changes*.

Is there something you have long wanted to do – a someday wish? Hold it in your mind for a little while.

Can anything be done today to bring that wish nearer fulfilment? Or maybe this is something that you should drop as an idea? Remember that abandoning a plan is alright too.

Just remember that unfulfilled *"someday ideas"* can hold us fast like wet sand and prevent us from making progress in many other areas. It lifts a heavy load off our shoulders when we finally decide to *"do it"* or *"dump it."*

Today is an opportunity to perform some action, any action, that will leave the world even a slightly better place by the time you go to bed tonight. Spend a short while thinking of what that action might be and figure out when and how you might do it – but please do it today.

The life of each of us causes ripples just like the ripples you see when you drop a stone into a calm lake. The Buddha says *"Whatever words we utter should be chosen with care, for people will hear them and be influenced by them for good or ill."*

TONY BRADY

A kind word, or a helpful deed starts a chain reaction of compassion. An unkind word cannot be taken back, uttering it is like ripping open a pillow full of feathers. So, for today resolve to speak only kind words and perform only kind actions, just for today. It makes a difference.

Some words from the Buddha to end this reflection:

> *"Just as a mother would guard her child,*
> *her only child, with her own life, even so,*
> *let me cultivate a boundless mind for all*
> *beings in the world.*
>
> *Let me cultivate a boundless love for all*
> *beings in the world, above, below, and*
> *across, unhindered, without ill will or*
> *enmity.*
>
> *Standing, walking, seated, or lying down,*
> *free from torpor,*
> *let me as far as possible*
> *fix my attention on this recollection.*
>
> *This, they say, is the divine life right*
> *here."*

16 - GRATITUDE FOR WATER

This meditation is designed to help you make use of water as a means of finding a place of calm. I hope it will help you discover and cultivate an area of flexibility in your life.

If possible, I encourage you to set up a room, or a corner of a room, as a place for regular quiet meditation. You need very little to furnish this space. You will always find that less is more in your meditation setup.

You might like to have in front of you a statue or image of the Buddha or Jesus or some inspirational figure. You could place there a simple flower, an incense holder.

I caution against using a live flame but if you decide to use a candle you know to take very particular extra care.

Some people like to have in front of them a picture of a loved one to whom they dedicate their meditation.

Whatever you select you will find it will help if you keep everything uncomplicated. The message, *keep it simple*.

For this exercise can I ask you to place on the table in front of you a plain, unadorned glass filled with drinking water. Then you are ready to begin.

A reflection on water from Thich Nhat Hahn - It is called *"Turning on the water."*

> *"Water comes from high mountain sources.*
> *Water runs deep in the Earth.*
> *Miraculously, water comes to us and sustains all life.*
> *My gratitude is filled to the brim."*

Take now a few moments to become more aware of your existence in the here and the now.

Try to ensure you are in comfortable position. Feet on the ground, back straight - but not rigid, hands joined on your lap or hands on your thighs.

Notice your body. Become aware of your breathing in and your breathing out. Notice the short gap that occurs between each in-breath and each out-breath.

Notice any feeling of tension, physical or mental, and see if by mindfully breathing in and out you can manage to release that tension. With practice you can do this.

A WAVE OF BLESSING AND OTHER MEDITATIONS

Remember all is well in these few moments. We have the time to do all we need to do. So take it easy. Slow down.

Next, bring your attention to the glass of water in front of you.

Notice its stillness. See if you can, for this little while, imitate the tranquillity that you observe in the water.

Notice the peace of that stillness. See if you can rest in that calm. Let the stillness of the water into your soul.

Recall how, if muddy water is allowed to settle, the mud will fall to the bottom. The image of still water will pacify your muddied mind. We learn not to stir up the dirt.

Give yourself a little time quiet where we try to reflect the peace of still water. Let the stillness of water speak to you.

We know water has wondrous power. Harnessed, it can turn turbines and generate electricity to power a city. Unleashed, the force of water can cause unimaginable destruction, as we have seen on our television screens.

We are like water. With our energy harnessed and controlled we can accomplish great good. With our power unleashed and out of control we are capable of terrible destruction. Water reminds us of our possibilities.

Reflect for a while on your water-like power for good or ill and resolve to harness your energy for what is called the *skillful way of life, the good life*. It is possible and very necessary in a world where the voices of conflict speak more stridently than the voices of peace.

Again bring your attention to the still water in the glass. Notice how, under the power of gravity, water adapts to its container whatever the shape of the vessel. Water is supremely flexible. Can you imitate the flexibility of water when you face unexpected changes in the pattern of your life? Water does not resist, water adapts.

Lao Tzu tells us *"Nothing is softer or more flexible than water, yet nothing can resist it."*

Perhaps reflect for a minute on how you might become more adaptable and more flexible – just like water.

And maybe if you can become more flexible yourself you might find that people will offer less resistance to you.

Finally, having observed the water before you, and having gained inspiration from it as to how you can do better, take a sip of this life-giving water, remembering that it is essential to all life on earth.

The health benefits of water are unquestioned. People who have clean water on tap sometimes take it for granted. We do not value it half enough. So many people in the world do not have access to clean drinking water. Many others have to trek for kilometres to reach it. The lucky people turn a tap, and fresh, clean water is there.

So, hold the glass in your hand, look at the water, really appreciate the wonderful gift that is before you. Give thanks for this stuff of life, this water that connects all humanity and every living thing that has ever lived on the Earth.

A closing thought:

May the gift of water remind us of the gifts which each of us brings to the world and our community,

May it prompt us to reflect with gratitude on the water that nourished us even before we were born,

May water continue to give us sustenance, energy and daily inspiration for our life's journey.

May we always thirst for justice and peace just as we thirst for water.

"Nothing in the world
is more flexible and yielding
than water.
Yet when it attacks the firm
and the strong, none can withstand it,
because they have no way to change it.
So the flexible overcome the adamant,
the yielding overcome the
forceful.
Everyone knows this,
but no one can do it."

Words of Lao Tzu

17 - A GRATITUDE WALK DOWN MEMORY LANE

Welcome to this reflection which is designed to lead you on a grateful walk down memory lane. I hope will leave you relaxed and with a feeling of thankfulness for many of the good things which have accompanied you on your journey of life.

But first you need to take a few seconds to come into this present astonishing moment, this temporary stopping point between past and future, the point in time where everything happens. So relax and let things be for now.

See if you can find or yourself a comfortable place where you will be less likely to be disturbed. Take in a mindful breath and allow yourself the opportunity to look within.

Breathing in and out, just notice in gratitude the fact that you are here, alive and aware in this present moment.

TONY BRADY

Naturally breathing in, and then breathing out, in grateful awareness of the here and the now.

A thought, "Slow me down" by Wilfred A. Peterson:

"Steady my hurried pace
with a vision of the eternal march of time.

Ease the pounding of my heart
by the quieting of my mind.

Give me amid the confusion of the day,
the calmness of the eternal hills.

Break the tension of my nerves
and muscles

with the soothing music of the singing
streams that live in my memory.

inspire me to send my roots deep into the
soil of life's enduring values

that I may grow toward the stars of my
greater destiny."

A WAVE OF BLESSING AND OTHER MEDITATIONS

Now take a step back in time to the time of your childhood.

Look back on the people who loved you and cared for you in your earliest days.

Think of the people who took care of you, who played and had fun with you, who were with you as you started to walk and talk. You could call these people the *Santa Claus People* of your early life.

Now relax for a while in the happy memory of these individuals and their kindnesses to you in your childhood.

Then you went through the right of passage and the difficulties and doubts of adolescence. In these times some people were close to you and helped you through the ups and downs of those tumultuous days.

There were times when you thought you knew it all, other times when you had the greatest of doubts, but you made it through in the end.

Now spend a while thinking of the people who put up with you and helped get you through this necessary and sometimes painful passage into adulthood.

Next, take a look back on your young adulthood when you began to establish your place in the world, school days over, working life starting, new relationships developing. Perhaps you moved out of your family home, maybe setting up a family of your own. As the song puts it *"Those were the days my friend, we thought they'd never end, we'd sing and dance forever and a day."*

Think of the people and circumstances who supported you as you set out and made your way into the brave new world of adulthood.

Next, take a little time to think about your benefactors of more recent times, the people who support you even now. Call to mind people whose care (and love) for you is so unquestioned that you might even take them for granted.

Stop to see if you can remedy that by giving thanks for the considerate people, the reliable people and all the good things that surround you day by day.

Relax for a minute of silent thanksgiving for all this, for a final moment of appreciation for your life in general. The fact that you are here. The fact that there is anything here rather than nothing at all. The wonder of our existence is a cause for endless gratitude. You can ask yourself *"why anything"* and then *"why me?."*

A WAVE OF BLESSING AND OTHER MEDITATIONS

Having been so inundated with goodness and blessing what can you do but resolve to offer kindness and care in return.

So resolve now to be fun and a delight to the young.

A reassurance to those enduring growing pains.

May you be a support to people in general, especially as life and fitness give way to older age.

Resolve to be a help to people as they struggle to let go. Constant change, allowing things to come and go , are facts of life that all of us must learn to accept. In coping with that, the support of others will help us. Let your mission in life be finding the happiness that comes by helping other people

Let's take some moment of quiet and calm as you near the conclusion of this reflection.

Notice your breathing.
Notice any sounds in the world around you.

Breathe out a sigh of happy contentment for all these good recollections before you return to the work of today.

A closing thought:

> *I expect to pass through this world but once. Any good, therefore, that I can do or any kindness I can show to any fellow creature, let me do it now. Let me not defer or neglect it for I shall not pass this way again.*

May every one of your activities inspire in you a feeling of gratitude for all the good things of your life.

May you find your life filled with ever more reasons for gratefulness.

18 - WHY KNOCK YOURSELF?

In this reflection, we ask *"Why do we keep knocking ourselves?"*

We habitually blame ourselves for what we may have done in the past.

We constantly criticise ourselves for what we may have left undone in the past.

How can we get it right?

Let us have a look and see if we can be a little more gentle on ourselves. Will this help us to move forward?

Begin by settling into a quiet state. Take in a deep breath. Hold for a second or two before gently letting it go.

Try that one more time:

TONY BRADY

Deep breath in - Hold - let it go.

Notice how that little exercise - and you can do it anywhere - will open the door to the present moment. Remember to open that door whenever you get an opportunity throughout the day.

A quote from the poet Shelly:

> *"In a drama of the highest order there is little food for censure or hatred; it teaches rather self-knowledge and self-respect."*

So back to our opening question — *"Why do we keep knocking ourselves?"*

It could be that we have made mistakes in the past. But ask yourself *"who hasn't made a mistakes?"*

We can learn from our mistakes. Mistakes can help us turn ourselves around. Sometimes our very best resolutions come from having made a blunder.

And not every slipup of the past is irredeemable or

catastrophic. For the few that are, we will gain nothing by beating ourselves with a stick. Let's look at what is causing our low self-esteem and see where we might turn this feeling into a spur, an encouragement for more wise and beneficial action in the future.

Take one minute for this little exercise - just 60 undisturbed seconds in which you ask *"Why do I knock myself?"*

Sometimes we disparage ourselves because we feel unworthy of love or kindness. This might have been drummed into us as children, perhaps in school or maybe even at home.

It is no harm to try to find the source of this discomfort. But also remember to notice just how far we have come since the days when these feelings of inadequacy were sown and took root in our minds.

See if you can forgive the people and the circumstances that caused you to feel this way. That is not always easy, but, in so far as we can pardon these situations, we will gain freedom from them. It is worth the effort to try.

Nelson Mandela reminds us *"As I walked out the door towards the gate that would lead to my freedom, I knew if I didn't leave my bitterness and hatred behind, I'd still be in prison."*

So it is with us, we forgive, and we move on.

Sometimes we knock ourselves down. When we beat ourselves up as inadequate, when we are harsh on ourselves, it is no harm to ask ourselves if would we even think for one moment of treating other people as harshly as we treat ourselves? Almost certainly the answer is that we would not. Instead, we might call even a difficult person to one side and encourage them by pointing out all their good attributes.

And remember that even the worst of us has some good characteristics that can be nurtured and brought to flower.

The flower that would have opened under the influence of the gentle warmth of softness and compassion closes tightly in the colder air.

So let us remember to treat ourselves and others to more than an occasional dose of kindness and compassion. It will be found to be worthwhile.

It is no harm also to remember that if we have a habit of judging ourselves harshly, we are very likely to begin to treat others the same way. In that way the pain caused by harsh treatment goes around and around.

Therefore, in the time ahead, be gentle with yourself and with others. Make up your mind that the time for harsh personal judgment of yourself, or anyone else for that matter, is over.

Call to mind the words of the poem *"Desiderata"* by Max Ehrmann:

> *"You are a child of the universe,*
> *no less than the trees and the stars;*
> *you have a right to be here."*

And, not forgetting the poem's encouraging final lines:

> *"Be cheerful.*
> *Strive to be happy."*

You can search throughout the entire universe for someone who is more deserving of your love and affection than you are yourself, and that person is not to be found anywhere. You yourself, as much as anybody in the entire universe deserve your love and affection.

Words of the Buddha

19 - WHEN WILL WE BE AWARE?

John Lennon who coined the memorable phrase *"Life is what happens to you when you're busy making other plans"* and is that not very accurate?

In this reflection, we will try to see if we can recover our awareness of life as it comes to us. Let us see if we can enter life in the present moment.

"Let us not look back in anger, nor forward in fear, but around in awareness." - James Thurber.

When I look back at my own life, I cannot fail to notice that it has mainly been a life lived in non-awareness. Assuredly, it has been a life lived in the present moment, but frantic for the most part with little time to stop and think along the way. I look back and ask myself in amazement "where have those years gone?" In recent years I have tried to become more mindful which is why you are reading this. But taken as a whole the moments of reflection have been disappointingly few and frighteningly sporadic.

But, undaunted we begin again today, you and I together.

Please begin by taking just a one minute pause to see if you can become aware of what is going on for you in this present moment. In this first pause concentrate on your body, your breathing, your heartbeat, your bodily sensations. For one minute give yourself a time in which to notice the gift of your existence in this time and place.

We live, move and have our being in an astonishing, indescribable, existence. Science has revealed a world of matter within and beneath what we can see with the naked eye. At the other end of the scale, we observe countless billions of stars in numberless billions of galaxies, worlds beyond counting, the stuff beyond imagination.

When on a clear night and away from the pollution of city lights, we observe the magic of the night sky, a magic that is only a tiny fraction of the amazement that lies beyond what we can see. Sometimes we trouble our minds with complaints about such every problems as traffic jams, and we can spend our days alternating between a frenzy of work and an orgy of consumerism. We are let with the extraordinary image of people working hard so that they can afford a break from work, people labouring extra hours so they can purchase labour saving devices.

I invite you to take another one minute pause to examine your relationship with work. Is it a healthy balance? Does it allow time and space for awareness of the fact that you are alive in a magical existence?

Next, you might go on to consider the people in your life. Your family, your friends, people you have worked with, people who have thought you valuable lessons of life. As you go through the list of people, ask yourself where each of these people will be 100 years from now.

I look out my window, and it is sobering to realise that not one person whose house is in my view will be here in that relatively short time. It is time to be kind to those around us. It is time to forgive any grievances. It is time to put aside any feelings of jealousy.

So what, if someone had a bigger house, a more hi-tech car, money for more exotic holidays. Look upon one and all with eyes of compassion. We all share this gift of life, and we will all, at some point in time, have the solitary experience of death. We each enter, and each of us will leave, this world alone. We need to be more aware of our shared humanity.

I suggest now a final one minute pause to allow you to give thanks for the people in your lives and resolve to take better notice and better care of them.

Our failures in awareness in the past need not be a discouragement to us. We can turn around and redirect our lives in one minute, even in this very second. Indeed, this is the only moment in which we can put our good intentions into effect. So, let us begin here and now.

Out closing thought for this reflection is a message of hope and encouragement from the Dali Lama:

> *"We are visitors on this planet. We are here for one hundred years at the very most. During that period, we must try to do something good, something useful, with our lives. If you contribute to other people's happiness, you will find the true meaning of life."*

20 - IN TIMES OF FEAR AND UNCERTAINTY

In times of fear, it can be harder to sit in meditation. Our minds are racing. At times we can feel downhearted and even depressed. When this happens, we can freeze into a mindless routine. We lose our sense of priorities. At these times we tend to do everything except the one essential thing that needs to be done right now.

But at times like this, we need to break the pattern by stopping and sitting. The sitting does not have to be for long, but we need to sit to break the downward spiral of fear, that inner anxiety that we cannot quite put the finger on but we feel it there in the pit of our stomach.

We do not want to stop, we are afraid to stand still, but we need to stop. We must stop.

This reflection is your invitation to sit and stop for a few moments where I hope you will rediscover and inner peace that will make a difference to your life.

TONY BRADY

So please now enter your calm space, the corner where you usually attempt your meditation practice.

Leave the phone to one side, sit in your quiet chair or take up position on your cushion, whatever makes you feel comfortable.

Breathe in

Breathe out

With each breath see if you can bring yourself to a more profound place of quiet within.

Just breathing in

Just breathing out

Leaving everything else to one side - just for now - all is well

May this time and place be a shelter for you.

When you come into this room may all the weight of the world fall from your shoulders.

May nothing destructive ever cross this threshold.

A WAVE OF BLESSING AND OTHER MEDITATIONS

In this place may you be tranquil, blessed by a peace that the world cannot give.

May this be a lucky place, A place where all your heart desires will find a pathway to your door.

Now take a one minute break, just one minute to step off the treadmill.

Zen Master Thich Nhat Hahn offers this advice:

"If we suffer, it is not because things are impermanent. It is because we believe things are permanent. When a flower dies, we don't suffer much. We understand that flowers are impermanent. But often we cannot accept the impermanence of a beloved one, and we suffer deeply when the person passes away."

Aware of impermanence, we become more positive, more loving and more wise.

Let us now send out thoughts of loving kindness to anyone who is currently finding difficulty with the pace of change in his or her own life. Remember too anyone suffering just from he general pace of change in life.

May all who face change today find the support they need to cope with that change.

May they find the courage to face the future with hope.

May they find the support they require in order to face the future without fear.

May all who face change today be free from all danger in their new situation.

May they be well in mind and body.

May all who face adjustments today find themselves in a place of ease and at peace.

I invite you to take a one minute pause in which you seek serenity, courage and wisdom.

May you be blessed with the serenity to accept the events in your life that you cannot change. May you have the courage to change the things you can and should change. May you have the wisdom to know the difference between the two.

When a disciple once asked the Sufi mystic Rumi: What is Fear? Rumi replied: *"Fear is non-acceptance of uncertainty. If we accept uncertainty, it becomes adventure."*

It can be frightening to abandon the familiar and the accustomed and to realise that we are not in control. Our anxiety doesn't come from thinking about the future. Our anxiety comes from wanting to control the future.

Attachment too, causes us to fear loss or change. We can be attached to people, to material things, to our jobs. But we must remember that *everything* changes. Human beings always share a finite time together.

Nobody knows when their shared time with someone else is going to come to an end. Some relationships will terminate because of changed circumstances. But finally all human relationships end when a loved one passes away.

Non-attachment enables us to live our relationships with love and joy and gratitude, knowing that they could end at any moment.

We often cling to pleasure, hoping that it will stay.

We are often overwhelmed by pain, fearing that it will never go away.

Non-attachment helps us to enjoy the beautiful moments without being plagued by the fear that they will end — as we know they will. - Non-attachment helps to endure the difficult moments knowing that *"this too shall pass"*.

Acceptance of change helps keep us balanced. In good times and bad, it is useful to recall those all-important words *"this too will pass."*

Fran Brady sums up our situation in these two lines:

> *"But who can hold the crimson dawn*
> *Or stop a sunset yielding to the night."*

A one minute pause now to see if we can resolve to be less attached in our dealings with other people and less attached to our worldly possessions.

Less attachment does not mean being less loving, less appreciative. Awareness and acceptance of uncertainty and change enhance our appreciation and our love.

A closing thought from Interfaith prayers and blessings by Abby Willowroot:

> *"May I come to understand that blessings are everywhere, that my attitude will affect outcomes, that challenges are often gifts in disguise.*
>
> *May I come to trust that most things can get better, with time, that my instincts and gut feelings have value, that a positive attitude makes things go smoother.*

May I come to see that I have many skills and talents I can use, that I am a positive influence on many people, that there are those around me who wish me well.

May I come to value that today is a blessing to be enjoyed, that each person is unique and important, that each moment of my life has meaning."

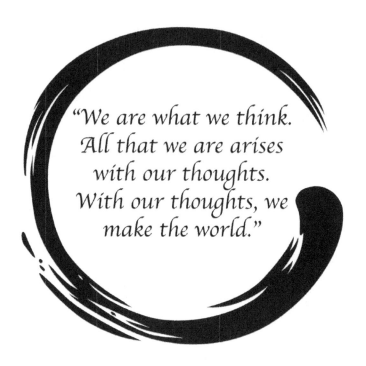

"We are what we think.
All that we are arises
with our thoughts.
With our thoughts, we
make the world."

Words of the Buddha

21 - YOU ARE A TODAY'S GIFT TO THE WORLD.

Welcome to this reflection the message of which is one of encouragement from realising that you are today's gift to the world.

You don't have to think of being the best you can be for a lifetime, for a year, for a week, or even for a day. Just be kind to the next person you meet, and then to the following person, and then to the person after that.

So, let us begin.

It would be good if you can establish a regular place and time for meditation.

If you have a room or a corner of a room that is great. Try for a place where, most of the time, you expect to be undisturbed. But don't let the thought of noise or intrusions stop you from making a start. It is hard to escape the din of the world, and, as for the interruptions, don't anticipate trouble. It may not happen.

And you don't have to meditate for long. Even five minutes a day is a start. Just as in the case of learning to play an instrument, it is better to practice for five minutes every day than to sit down for a one hour (or more) marathon session every week.

Always begin by making sure you are in a comfortable position. See if you can relax. Quieten your busy mind.

For these few minutes leave to one side the cares of the day. Later on, there will be time enough for attending to the to-do list.

For the next two minutes, just relax, rest, be still. If you lose concentration, return to your place of rest. No pressure, that is why this is called a practice.

An opening thought from the Buddha:

> *"You can search throughout the entire universe for someone who is more deserving of your love and affection than you are yourself, and that person is not to be found anywhere. You yourself, as much as anybody in the entire universe deserve your love and affection."*

Our life is made up of minutes; it comes to us a second at a time, our heartbeats come one at a time. In the average lifetime, the human heart beats nearly three and a half billion times. But these beats come one at a time, second by second, a constant trickle.

In the same way, our lives can be a constant trickle of goodness. Being kind in the next second may not seem a great deal but just imagine if any of us could at the end of our lives look back at three billion seconds of kindness. That would be something extraordinary.

If you consider the year ahead, the idea of maintaining a resolution can seem to be quite challenging. But then, when you glance back and reflect upon the last year, you can see how quickly time has actually passed.

Every day has offered an opportunity for doing good. The question we have to consider is *"How have we responded to that invitation?"*

The good news is that every day offers us the same opportunity.

Why not now spend two minutes in quiet reflection on time, the time of your life.

Ask what you might do with time in future when you consider the use you have made of it so far?

TONY BRADY

Mary Oliver tells us:

*Tell me, what is it you plan to do with
your one wild and precious life?*

*When it's over, I want to say: all my life
I was a bride married to amazement. I
was the bridegroom, taking the world into
my arms*

*Instructions for living a life. Pay
attention. Be astonished. Tell about it.*

*To pay attention, this is our endless and
proper work.*

*I don't want to end up simply having
visited this world.*

At this point, a pause is appropriate, just one minute to be spent in simple gratitude for your being and considering how that gratitude might be expressed in action.

So now that you are in your chair think of the people you are likely to encounter today.

Remember to face the day with newness. Much of the time we tend to approach the day on autopilot. When we are on autopilot, we do not notice the good that inundates us from all sides. We react, sometimes wrongly, when things go against us. We lose our temper in traffic. We are impatient with people we meet. We fail to respect our work colleagues. We take family members for granted.

This period of reflection gives you an opportunity to reduce any inbuilt tendency to operate on autopilot. You think ahead. You prepare yourself to deal with life's inevitable challenges in a constructive way.

You set out intending to do a good deed, looking to do good, with the intention of creating opportunities to put kindness into effect and to put your best foot forward.

At this stage take another one minute pause for reflection.

Never underestimate the value of each positive action. Proceeding from even one person, kindness and generosity are infectious. Someone is kind to us and, in our gratitude, we want to be generous to someone else, and so the positive feeling goes around and around. Even the ripples from one everyday good deed can lift person after person until everyone experiences an uplift.

In the same way, irritability and ill will can bring us all down in ways that we can hardly begin to imagine.

We are all human of course, and it is inevitable that on some occasions we will be in an irritable frame of mind. If so, we must strive to show little trace of it, for nothing is more infectious than ill humour.

There is the wise advice to count to ten when you find yourself in poor form. Better still would be to get out of the way if you possibly can.

When irritation arises, take a few minutes to reflect and to settle yourself.

When you are annoyed with someone, it helps if you can stop and consider *"where will we all be in 10, 20, 30 or more years?"* You know that the answer will be *"Almost certainly not looking as good as we do today"* and some of us maybe even returned to the good earth from which we came.

As yourself *"How significant will this difference of opinion be in the story of my life?"*

It helps if you can somehow, even in the heat of the moment, manage to take a breath, pause any tendency to react and see if you can manage to put any differences into perspective.

A WAVE OF BLESSING AND OTHER MEDITATIONS

Now an invitation to enjoy one minute of peaceful reflection before this closing thought which comes from Kalidasa:

"Look to this day:
For it is life, the very life of life.

In its brief course
Lie all the verities and realities of your
existence.

The bliss of growth,
The glory of action,
The splendour of achievement
Are but experiences of time.

For yesterday is but a dream
And tomorrow is only a vision;

And today well-lived makes
Yesterday a dream of happiness

And every tomorrow a vision of hope.
Look well therefore to this day;

Such is the salutation to the ever-new dawn!"

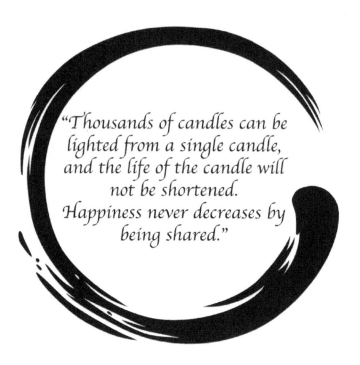

"Thousands of candles can be lighted from a single candle, and the life of the candle will not be shortened. Happiness never decreases by being shared."

Words of the Buddha

22 - YOU ARE UNIQUE

This period of quiet reflection is designed to remind you of the unique person you are. Yes, you are only one of the seven billion people on earth but understand this for sure, you *are* unique and irreplaceable.

An opening thought:

I come into this quiet space to remind me to rest for a moment on the forming edge of my life.

To resist the headlong tumble into the next moment, until I claim for myself awareness and gratitude,

Until I take the time to look out into the great world around me and see in that world a community awaiting my unique contribution,

So I invite you now to just become aware of your presence in this room at this time. Really arrive here. Be present.

TONY BRADY

Notice your breath.

Breathe in - breathe out

Place your hand on your chest.

Notice your heartbeat giving life.

And for just for a few seconds experience a feeling of gratitude for being here, a sensation of thankfulness for these quiet moments of reflection and contemplation.

Your existence here is something quite remarkable.

As you know you are composed of billions upon billions of atoms and subatomic particles which somehow come together to make you the person you are.

Bill Bryson in his book "A brief history of nearly everything" make this interesting observation: "*If someone took a tweezers and removed atom after atom until all your atoms were arranged in a single heap he would be left with a heap of atoms, none of which is living or conscious, but which in their previous state of togetherness went to make you who you are, a living, thinking, conscious being.*"

This reminds us that people are much more than the total of their parts.

For that, we should be profoundly thankful, so I invite you to spend some time in a state of gratitude for the wonder of your being.

Next, it might be useful to realise that you and I, your combination of atoms reading this and my mixture of molecules putting this reflection together, are like all people, amazingly, entirely and utterly unique.

You are here now, no one in the whole world is exactly like you.

No one has ever been the same as you, and no one will ever be just like you.

You are a one-off.

No other person has your unique life experience; no one has your exact talents, your skills, your feelings.

Your life and your existence are truly beyond belief.

Please rest for a while in thankfulness for the astounding fact of your uniqueness. We do not allow ourselves enough of these quiet moments to appreciate the wonder of who we are.

Our distinctiveness means that no one can do precisely the things that you can do. No other person can participate in society in the way that you can contribute in this short life during which your unique combination of atoms holds together. This life represents your unique popping into being and your chance to play your distinctive part in the history of this marvellous universe.

As Tony Lloyd puts it *"What will you do with this one short, amazing life?"*

Here take another pause for reflection.

Just think of the combinations of couplings reaching back over centuries, over millennia which finally resulted in your being born to your parents.

Any break in that sequence, any slight change in timing, any different sperm being the first to make contact with any waiting egg and someone else would be reading this reflection and not you.

Of course, any such change of history on my side would mean that no one would be reading this particular moment of contemplation because, just like you, I would not be here.

Our presence here is amazing and to be aware of it is awe inspiring. With all our faults we are extraordinary, and with mindfulness, we can, hopefully, minimise the less attractive aspects of our character.

Our closing thought is from GK Chesterton:

> *"Here ends another day, during which I have had eyes, ears, hands and the great world around me. Tomorrow begins another day. Why am I allowed two?"*

Why indeed.

Why was I even allowed one?

Now, what will I do with this one, short, wondrous life?

Words from the Native American Tradition

"Hold on to what is good,
Even if it's a handful of earth.
Hold on to what you believe,
Even if it's a tree that stands by itself.
Hold on to what you must do,
Even if it's a long way from here.
Hold on to your life,
Even if it's easier to let go.
Hold on to my hand,
Even if someday I'll be gone away
from you."

23 - TAKE BACK YOUR ON-LINE LIFE

This meditation aims to help you take back some of that part of your life which you spend online.

Life is short, and when it is over, we would like to think our friends might have something more significant to say about us than the fact that we responded to our emails by return or that we always kept up to date with the news.

These humdrum life activities are not usually place highly on lists of regrets felt by people who are dying.

But have no fear. This invitation to notice our online distractions is not an exhortation to return to some imagined golden pre-digital age. We are where we are.

But first, come into the present moment - spend the next minute of silence re-connecting with your breath becoming aware of the gift of your existence in the here and the now.

TONY BRADY

This opening thought is a variation of a prayer from Paul Stephan Dodenhoff:

"For these next few moments,
Spirit of Life we let go.

For these next few moments
may we let go of our anxieties,

our fears,

our anger,

our self-doubts,

our regrets,

our petty grievances,

and our distractions.

May these next few moments,

light our way to peace and serenity."

How often do we go online to do a simple task and find ourselves getting drawn into a larger and larger pool of information and distraction? Every second thing we come across seems like a good idea, something else to add to the ever growing to do list, something to do, a film to see, a book to read, a home improvement idea.

With newspapers and TV online, the news comes at us from across the interconnected globe, and we find ourselves exposed to an inundation of information about events over which we have no control.

This barrage of only-sometimes-useful information distracts us and disturbs our ability to work on the things in life which are within our power.

I invite you to spend one minute reflecting on how you manage to lose track of time when you allow yourself to fall into this black hole of information.

Now there are benefits to our being online and connected. This ability to link up with others is a potential source of immense good. Just think of how many good causes have reached a favourable conclusion through the co-operation of people who otherwise would never have known or met one another.

But really how much of our online time do we spend in actively doing what we can for the causes which are near and dear our hearts? If you are like me, I suspect that much of what we take in goes in one ear and out the other without giving rise to any constructive action. Just ask yourself *"How much of my daily browsing can I recall even ten minutes afterwards?* How useful has that been?

It is time to spend a minute or two examining your routine relationship with the media and seeing if there is any indication of a problem requiring a solution.

I have experimented with different ways of coping with my tendency to spend too many valueless hours looking at screens. I have tried the idea of one tech-free day per week and found it impossible to manage. So many of our everyday tasks involve online activity, from diaries to weather forecasts and checking timetables, not to mention meditation apps. All of this makes the idea of a weekly tech-free day impossible for me, and I suspect for many other people.

Then there was the idea of a half-day tech-fast. I regret to report that the half-day tech-fast idea did not fare much better.

So where better to look for a solution than online? There are apps which act as a reminder of how long you have been online, and they offer the opportunity of automatically cutting you off. These apps would be excellent if you only had one device, but they do not operate manageably in a world where we each have portable as well as fixed devices.

The solution that I offer to you (and to myself) is easier, it does not require online help, and it operates over multiple devices:

The idea is that you would first ask yourself what you feel is a reasonable amount of time that you might usefully spend online. I am taking here about leisure time rather than work time which might of necessity involve being online. I mean limiting time devoted to the news, the checking of our social media and general browsing. (Emails are of a different order and require attention according to their importance)

Having fixed that maximum browsing time then make use of a simple cooking timer to notify you when the time limit is up. You do not need another high-tech gadget, you already have enough of these. You can split the allotted time into multiple shorter sessions if you wish.

Remembering that the work will expand to fill the time available this timing will have the effect of concentrating your mind and ensuring that you spend your online time as usefully as possible

Now see if you can take a minute to work out in your mind whether or not this might work for you and how you might put your solutions into effect beginning even today. Jot down a note of your plan and see how it works. It is not written in stone. It will be a case of trial and error but unless you make a plan you will never get your online time under control.

I hope this reflection has given you some food for thought and that it will gain you some valuable minutes, hours or days to add to the amazing gift that is your life.

In conclusion a thought from Seneca, the Roman philosopher who lived around the time of Christ. The following is one of his quotes on the Shortness of Life:

> *"You live as if you were destined to live forever, no thought of your frailty ever enters your head, of how much time has already gone by you take no heed. You squander time as if you drew from a full and abundant supply, though all the while that day which you bestow on some person or thing is perhaps your last."*

24 - A WAVE OF BLESSING

The poet-priest John O'Donohue make the point that each one of us has the power to bless. The act of blessing is not uniquely a priestly function. Each of our lives can be a blessing to others, and all our words can transmit love and comfort.

John describes a blessing as a circle of light drawn around a person to protect, heal and strengthen.

In this reflection, I hope we can create a circle of light and a wave of compassion that will gain momentum as it flows over each one of us. As it leaves each of us, it let it roll on to embrace others until our wave of kindness rises and breaks over the most distant shore. May the sun never set on our love.

Here is a blessing for you inspired by the Canticle of the Sun which is a canticle attributed to St Francis:

TONY BRADY

You may know the opening lines of the canticle:

"Sun and moon bless the Lord

Stars of the heavens bless the Lord"

And so, my blessing for you today:

May you be blessed by the warmth of the sun.

May you be comforted by the moon's light.

May you be inspired by the twinkling stars of the night.

May every day find you rising with gratitude,

And every night see you falling into a contented sleep.

May the snow, and the rain, fall gently upon you,

May the wind guide you safely home.

May water refresh your body and spirit.

A WAVE OF BLESSING AND OTHER MEDITATIONS

May you have food to eat,

And friends to accompany you on life's way.

In winter may you have fire to keep you warm,

Cool breezes to comfort you in summer,

A bed in which you find rest,

Shelter over your head.

May you experience joy in nature,

From the green grass

To the blue sky,

And, above, below, and to the right and left of you, the numberless array of creatures with whom we share this good earth.

May the works of humanity lead you to astonishment as you marvel at such things as:

TONY BRADY

The inventions of human ingenuity,

The conquering of disease,

The discoveries of science,

May you find inspiration in the lives of the most exceptional people who ever lived.

May you be comforted by the example set by all those who have overcome difficulty and suffering.

May you have just a little sorrow to help you understand the pain of others,

Just enough shortage to remind you to express gratitude for your abundance,

Just a small amount of disappointment so you can offer support to people whose lives have only a little light, perhaps only your light.

But may you never have so much trouble as will make you bitter or frustrated.

A WAVE OF BLESSING AND OTHER MEDITATIONS

May old age come upon you gently as the crowning of loved-filled days.

May death only come to you when your life's work is complete.

May you be blessed all of your days.

May the memory of you be an inspiration to all who have known and loved you.

In conclusion another thought from John O'Donohue:

> *"If you send out goodness from yourself, or if you share that which is happy or good within you, it will all come back to you multiplied ten thousand times. In the kingdom of love, there is no competition; there is no possessiveness or control. The more love you give away, the more love you will have."*

TONY BRADY

ABOUT THE AUTHOR

Tony Brady lives with his wife Fran, an environmental activist, in Dublin, Ireland. He has had a long time interest in spirituality and in particular in the Buddhist approach to life. He is the founder of, and regularly facilitates, a monthly Meetup group in Dublin dedicated to the practice of Buddhist Ethics. His contributions to the Insight Timer Meditation App have been listened to more than a quarter of a million times. He has recently been endorsed by the Irish Institute of Celebrants as a Professional Funeral Celebrant and he offers personalised funeral and memorial ceremonies at www.civil-funerals-dublin.com

A final word:

Treat the earth well.
It was not given to you by your parents,
it was loaned to you by your children.
We do not inherit the Earth from our Ancestors,
we borrow it from our Children.

(Native American tradition)

Made in United States
North Haven, CT
19 February 2023